WRITTEN BY MATT CROSSICK
ILLUSTRATED BY RICHARD JONES
DESIGNED BY NIKKI KENWOOD

CONSULTANT: RICHARD JONES

First published by Parragon in 2007

Parragon
Queen Street House
4 Queen Street
Bath BA1 1HE, UK

ISBN 978-1-4054-9517-2
Printed in China

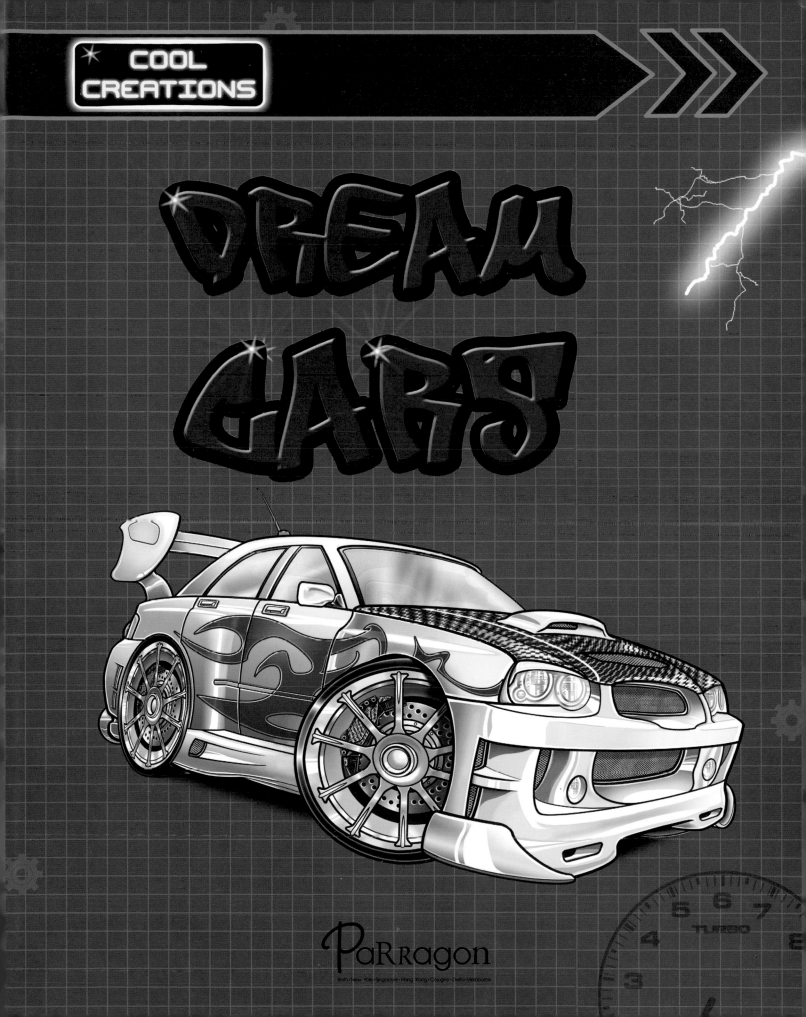

HOW IT WORKS

INSTALLING AND RUNNING YOUR CD-ROM

Check out the cool customizing ideas in this book, then follow the instructions below and get ready to start designing some hot rides on your **CD-ROM.**

USING A PC:

1. Put the CD into the CD drive.
2. Double click on "my computer."
3. Double click on the CD drive icon, "Dream Cars."
4. Double click on the "start pc" icon.

You will see a loading icon and your CD will start.

USING APPLE MACINTOSH®:

1. Put the CD into the CD drive.
2. Double click on the CD drive icon, "Dream Cars."
3. Double click on the "start osx" icon if running on an **OSX** system or "start classic" if running on **OS 9.2.**

You will see a loading icon and your CD will start.

This **CD-ROM** will work on most **PCs** or Apple Macintosh® computers. Please consult the system requirements on the next page for detailed specifications.

PC: WINDOWS® 98 / 2000 / ME / XP

- Win98, Pentium II processor / Win2000, WinXP, WinME Pentium III processor
- CD-ROM drive
- Sound card
- Monitor displaying at least 800 x 600 pixels in 256 colors or higher
- 128MB of Ram (256 MB recommended)

APPLE MACINTOSH®: CLASSIC / OSX

- Power Macintosh G3 500 MHz or higher
- Running a minimum OS 9.2 / recommended Mac OS X 10.2.6, 10.3, 10.4
- CD-ROM drive
- Sound card
- Monitor displaying at least 800 x 600 pixels in 256 colors or higher
- 128 MB of Ram (256 MB recommended)

TECHNICAL DATA
Now you're ready to create your dream car. Just follow the directions on the **CD-ROM**. If you get stuck, click on the "Help" button on the screen.

YOUR MISSION

These cars don't look anything special—yet. Choose a motor, then get ready to turn it into one of the coolest rides on the planet!

RALLY CAR

Rally cars are built for off-road racing. They're great at spinning and sliding around tight corners, and they can tear about in mud without a problem.

DRAGSTER

Dragsters are made for one thing: To blast along in a straight line at top speeds. Give your dragster a great big engine and a parachute to help it stop!

SP

3

2

STR

This str
look ord
now, but
upgraded
some cool
panels, a b
and a new p
this could be
dream machi

LIMOUSIN

If you're going to bu
a limo, you'll need a
smooth ride, black
tinted windows, and
everything from TV
screens to supersonic
speakers inside. They
are for VIPs, after all!

Turn over the page to find out how you can make your car KING OF THE ROAD!

SPEED & POWER

AWESOME ENGINES

Every hot car needs a big, powerful engine. Check out these engines and choose the one that best suits the car that you've chosen.

V8 ENGINE

The **V8** engine is popular for fast street cars and dragsters. It has 8 cylinders (twice as many as a normal car) and is very powerful—perfect for quick acceleration and high top speeds.

V12 ENGINE

With even more cylinders than the **V8**, these engines are for super-cars and race cars only. These big power plants rev up to really high speeds, but they're fine-tuned and need a lot of looking after.

BOXER ENGINE

This 4-cylinder engine isn't as strong or as big as the **V8**, but it is very light. If you add a turbo for extra boost, this engine can turn a normal street car into a lightweight, nimble rally car.

COOL CHARGERS

Once you've chosen your engine, you can give it an extra power boost by adding a turbo or a supercharger. These gadgets blast more air into the engine cylinders, making the whole engine more powerful.

TURBOCHARGER

This clamps onto your engine and forces more air into the cylinders. It can add a lot of power to your car, but it only kicks in when you're already going quite fast.

TECHNICAL DATA

A good turbo can add hundreds of bhp (brake horsepower) to your car's stats and speed it up to hundreds of miles per hour!

TWIN TURBO

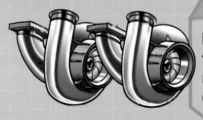

Double the turbos, double the fun! Having two turbos doesn't just give your car a mega boost though, it also makes your car run more smoothly.

SUPERCHARGER

Another way of boosting your engine power is to fit a supercharger to it. This sucks air from a scoop in the bonnet and blasts it into the cylinders, increasing your car's speed.

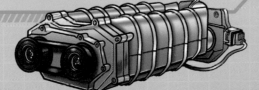

NEW ENGINE CHIP

Modern high-tech engines use computer technology to make sure they run smoothly. By adding a new, power-boosting chip, you can make it run faster without even using a wrench!

SPEED & POWER

SCORCHIN' EXHAUSTS/EXTRAS

If you've caught the power bug, you'll want to squeeze every last drop out of your engine—and that means upgrading the little things, too.

SPORTS EXHAUST

An upgraded exhaust doesn't just make your car sound loud, it also adds power to your engine by getting rid of the waste gases more quickly.

FUEL INJECTION

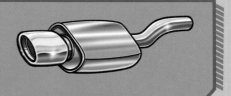

Modern engines use fuel injection to fire gasoline into the engine cylinders. The flow of gas is controlled by computer technology to get maximum power.

SIDE EXHAUST PIPES

These stylish exhaust pipes poke out sideways on each side of the car. They add power to the engine but, best of all, they look totally awesome!

AIR SCOOP

Engines need two things: gasoline and air. A big air scoop on the hood will force cool air into the cylinders, meaning more power. PLUS, it lets other drivers know that this car means speed.

RIP-ROARIN' RACING GEAR

By now you should have an engine, all souped up and ready to drive fast. Here are a few extreme add-ons that can turn your ride into a racing monster!

CARBON BRAKES

These great big discs squeeze against the wheels, clamping them hard and slowing the car down. Normal brakes can stop working when they get too hot, but carbon brakes work all race long.

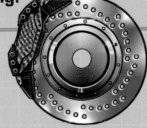

POWER GAS

This bottle of special gas links into your engine to give your car a HUGE 150 bhp boost, blasting it forward at hundreds of mph!

ROLL CAGE

Racing is a dangerous business. So if you're serious, you'll need a frame made of strong steel bars to protect you if your car flips over.

PARACHUTE

Drag racers can reach over 300 mph during a race. To stop quickly, you'll need a parachute that fires out of the back of your car to slow it down.

13

SMOOTH SHAPES

BRILLIANT BODY PANELS

Now that you've got the speed, you need the looks to match. Select different body parts for your car to make it a unique, custom-made machine!

CARBON-FIBER HOOD

Having a carbon-fiber hood makes a car lighter and faster, and it looks ultra-cool, too. This hood has a scoop in it to suck cool air into the engine.

MINI SIDE SCOOP

Racing brakes get so hot during a race, they can catch fire. So cool air blowing on them from a side scoop is vital.

SIDE SKIRT

These thin strips fit under your car doors to make the vehicle look low and mean. Some of the hottest modified cars are so low they almost scrape the ground!

BIG BUMPER

You can make your car look lower, faster, and meaner with a cool bumper. It keeps the front of the car close to the road, and it scoops up air to cool down the brakes and engine.

SUPER-COOL SPOILERS

When cars go over 100 mph, they want to take off. Spoilers help to push the back of the car down onto the road and give it extra grip around tight corners.

DRAGSTER SPOILER

A dragster can hit over 300 mph and, to keep a car stuck to the track at that speed, you need a big wing on the back.

STYLISH SPOILER

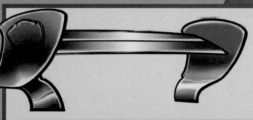

Although this spoiler does help to keep the car steady at high speeds, it's mainly just for show.

SUPER-CAR SPOILER

This hi-tech spoiler automatically pops up when the car goes over 100 mph and sinks back into the bodywork when the car slows down.

MINI SPOILER

Mini spoilers are secured to small or luxurious cars so that they don't interfere with the look of the vehicle. They look great on a limo.

PAINT & GRAPHICS

PAINT COLORS AND DAZZLIN' DECALS

By now you should have a fast car with a big engine and a cool custom shape. So what's next? A great paint job and decals, that's what!

TECHNICAL DATA
Decals are cool transfers and designs that you can put on your car once it has been painted.

BLINGIN' BLACK

The baddest-looking cars always seem to be black! They look dark, mean, and cool. Perfect for a limo!

FIERY FLAMES

Flame decals are one of the coolest types of design. They look really good on a red or black paint job and they show everyone that your car is the hottest on the road!

RALLY RACER

RACER LOGOS

Logos and transfers are usually used on race cars. These decals let other drivers know the name of the race team and their sponsors. Check out the fun logos on your **CD-ROM** by clicking on "View decal logos" at the bottom of the decals panel.

MULTICOLORS

Sports cars look extra sporty with super-bright body colors and even brighter, contrasting colors for the body panels.

PAINT & GRAPHICS

AWESOME WINDOWS

It's no good creating an amazing paint job, choosing some cool decals, and finishing off your design with a plain window—so why not go for tinted glass instead?

TINTED GLASS

Black tinted windows can look awesome. However, it's best not to choose them if you're making a race car. Pro drivers need clear windows for a good view of the race track.

NET WINDOW

Some race cars, such as dragsters, don't have side windows, so they might have a net window instead. This saves on weight, making the car faster, and won't shatter in a crash, like glass.

SUPER-COOL LIGHTS

Create some funky, colored headlights, then add other great light features to your ride.

NEON LIGHTS

These bright lights fit underneath your car to cast a futuristic glow around your engine. Perfect for modified street machines.

TECHNICAL DATA
Don't overload your car with extras if it looks cool already. You don't want to overdo it!

RALLY LIGHTS

If you're building the ultimate rally car, try adding a row of racing lights on the bumper. They're bright enough to light up a muddy track in the dark and look cool, too.

INTERIOR STYLE

COOL SCREENS & OTHER IN-CAR ENTERTAINMENT

Your car is almost finished, but there's one area that still needs customizing—the inside! Check out the cool screens, music tracks, speakers, and amps that best suit your ride.

TV SCREEN

PLASMA SCREEN

In a blinged-out car, a television is a major must-have item. Choose from a plasma screen that fits in your trunk, a fold-down screen that sits in your dashboard, or a small screen that can entertain your guests in the back of the car.

FOLD-DOWN SCREEN

SMALL SCREEN

SATELLITE NAVIGATION

Forget dusty old road maps—find the quickest way to your destination with a cool navigational system that fits into your dashboard. You'll be the king of the road in no time.

MUSIC TRACKS

First of all, you need to pick a tune that suits your ride. A big bass track is perfect for cruising along in a limo, while a fast techno beat will draw attention to a blinged-up street car.

AMPS AND SPEAKERS

An amplifier is an electronic box that powers a big speaker, and a big speaker means big noise. Modified cars have speakers in the doors and over the back seats. But your car isn't just modified, it's souped up to the hilt! Have fun adding amps and speakers to your car trunk to make it the ultimate extreme machine.

TRUNK VIEW

INTERIOR STYLE

STYLISH SEATS & STEERING WHEELS

Finally, the last step in building your blinged-up ride is to choose some seats and a steering wheel.

LIMO SEATS

These big leather seats are like armchairs. They'll help to prevent your body from aching if you've been driving all day.

RACING SEATS

These seats are light and strong, and support your body when you're flying around corners. They're called "bucket" seats and are built for race cars.

6 7
TURBO
8
9

TECHNICAL DATA

Race cars have very special interiors. There's no ICE (in-car entertainment), no fabric, no back seats—in fact, they're almost empty inside. This is to save weight, which makes the car faster.

STEERING WHEELS

A custom steering wheel is the finishing touch to a modified car. Some of the coolest cars have controls for high-tech gear, such as a power gas button that makes the car go faster.

TECHNICAL DATA

There's so little space inside a dragster that the driver needs to remove the steering wheel to climb into his seat, before slotting it back in again.

BACKDROPS

Pick a backdrop that suits your car. Remember that dragsters can't go around corners and low-down cruising cars would get stuck on a snowy rally course.

RALLY TRACK

This hilly track is perfect for tough rally cars. They can skid around corners, accelerate fast on straight roads, jump over bumps, and slide through the mud.

PERFECT FOR: Rally cars

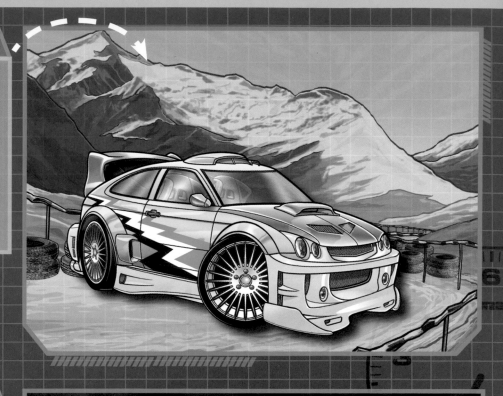

DRAG STRIP

This is a 1/4 mile long strip of road, where two cars accelerate as fast as they can in a straight line. Races last under ten seconds, but these powerful cars can reach up to 300 mph.

PERFECT FOR: Dragsters

CITY HARBOR

A big city with neon lights, tall buildings, and wide streets. It's the perfect place for showing off your dream ride during a chilled-out cruise!

PERFECT FOR: Limos

SHOWROOM

If you've built a show car to compete in modified car competitions, choose a special showroom backdrop, with spot lights pointing out its best features!

PERFECT FOR:
Modified street cars

Once you've created and printed out a custom-made dream machine for each car, why not make a copy of these two pages! Cut out the stat cards and keep them with your designs to remind you of their vital statistics!

SOUPED-UP STREET CAR

Top speed: **180 mph**

0–60 mph: **5 sec**

Power: **450 bhp**

Speed Rating: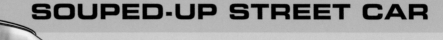

Style Rating:

DAZZLIN' DRAGSTER

Top speed: **300 mph**

0–60 mph: **1 sec**

Power: **1,500 bhp**

Speed Rating:  **Style Rating:**

LUXURY LIMOUSINE

Top speed: 140 mph
0–60 mph: 8 sec
Power: 250 bhp

Speed Rating: ⭐⭐   **Style Rating:** 🔥🔥🔥

RACING RALLY CAR

Top speed: 170 mph
0–60 mph: 2 sec
Power: 300 bhp

Speed Rating: ⭐⭐⭐⭐   **Style Rating:** 🔥🔥🔥